ALL THE SHADOWS CAST LIGHT

All the Shadows Cast Light
© 2025 Annina Melissa Published by Story Haus Press

All rights reserved. No part of this publication may be reproduced, distributed, or transmitted in any form or by any means, including photocopying, recording, or other electronic or mechanical methods, without the prior written permission of the publisher, except in the case of brief quotations used in critical reviews and other noncommercial uses permitted by copyright law.

For permission requests, contact: anninamelissa.com

ISBN: 978-1-0369-2801-8

Cover and interior illustrations © 2025 Annina Melissa Typography and design by Annina Melissa

Printed in United Kingdom

First edition, 2025

For all who wander.
And for T & M R, with love.

"One does not become enlightened by imagining figures of light, but by making the darkness conscious."

— *C.G. Jung*

Table of Contents
Lighter Things

All The Shadows Cast Light • 1
A World Of My Own • 3
The Match That Couldn't Sway • 5
Refraction • 9
The Escapist • 13
Exhibition Of Death • 15
I've Seen It All • 17
Before The First Touch • 21
Quiet Skulked Upon The Hour • 23
Riptide • 25
Trailblazer • 27
Sonder • 31
Echoes • 33
Firestarter • 35
Horned Women • 37
Shy Glimmers • 39

Silent Waters • 41

Fears • 45

To Stand Tall When Feeling Small • 47

Abalone • 49

Brush Strokes • 51

I Only Run With Myself • 53

Völva • 55

Mother • 57

Ode To The Sea • 61

Hourglass • 65

When The Marks Have Fallen • 67

Ahead • 69

All The Shadows Cast Light

All the shadows cast light
And all calamities aid
There's a crack in the wall
In the dimmest crusade
Scope for faith unbroken
Every step unafraid
Hope for words outspoken
Comfort in the shade

A World Of My Own

Window eyes
Conjuring nature
Bended matter
Quaint portraiture

Copious views
Internally strung
Force of expression
With no native tongue
But mindful alchemy
And grand illusions
Creating imagery
Guiding conclusions

Magic wit
And absent sense
Dawning mindscape
Proven defense
Lands of visions
And untamed creation
Friends and creatures
Of imagination

Window eyes
Constructed from wishbone
Unendingly craving
A world of my own

The Match That Couldn't Sway

Thin ropes
Incongruous cords
Ties which tied me down

Drawstrings
Sewn into toiled scraps
Old, ill-fitting gown

Ships of relation
Ships of friends
Sunk amidst the ocean

Hidden rocks
And undertows
Awaiting swift back motion

Ideas of no use
Beliefs which don't serve
Memories of toiled recollection

In brighter light
The brink of horizons
Never nests with abjection

Light-heartedly I lit
The match that couldn't sway
And all the bridges I burn
Glaringly light my way

ANNINA MELISSA

Refraction

Staring into the void
The unknown expanding beneath my feet
And with every step I take
I'm treading on what I can't defeat

Thin
On the ground
Cynical voices
Rail at the sound
Of every possibility
That outran their own choices

But in fear we are blind
Paralyzed
We're absolutized
In case what we had been looking for
Is not what we found
In case the pages of our lives
Had simply been misbound

And we had dared too much
And roamed too far
And flew too high
Forfeiting who we are
Tucked in the certainty of our regimes
Laughing away our unrealised dreams
Until we drown our pain in denial
And become bitter

I stare into the void
The unknown expands beneath my feet
'Thin on the ground',
He said
'Are the eyes which were scarred by illusion
Yet remain to see beyond what others believe to be dead'

And I wonder
Do you stare into me
The way I do into this abyss?
When in my head
Words unsaid
Entangle with memories of bliss
What do you conceive
Of the debris
That has now become a mere opaque vision
Of who we hoped to be?

How come you see through my skin
Like birefringent crystals but never beneath?
Polarized
And contradicting the obvious
Hollow marrow
Is this all you perceive?
I followed the afterglow
Until the shadow blinded me

I stare into the void
The unknown expanding beneath my feet
And with every step
I'm taking the lead

The Escapist

Where have you vaporised into, spirit?
Hollow the shell whose existence remains buried
And yet with love so pure
I felt touch where there was none
In the darkness cradled amongst dirt and stone
I became so bright the shadows fell behind me
I became so light I slipped right through
The grasp of the weight of the world

But wandering still in all that hope held tight
I can't find you, soul
I can't see the light
Yet lying still in all
Which was never meant to be
Where have you escaped to, breath?
Painted over with pretence
Bliss conquered ignorance

Exhibition Of Death

If there is no pain
How can there be bliss?
I'm clinging to what I collected so dearly
I want to believe
Origin dismissed
This womb I creep out of is nearly
Dying

And I dig deeper
Placing my fingertips on stardust
Cleansing my skin from rust
And I dig deeper
Placing my vision into hope
Witnessing liberation
And I dig deeper
Until every fractal realigns
Inconsistency's synchronized
Abnegation aphorised
Life internalized

I've Seen It All

I've seen two wrongs make a right
And darkness illuminating light
And blind eyes clearing a pall

I've seen victims without cases
And footsteps without traces
And voices proclaim they've heard it all

I've seen years wasted on the young
And old fools rolling youth of their tongue
Choosing to not answer time's pressing call

I've seen cures without cause
And reticence without pause
A new day dawning during nightfall

I've seen psychosis with my own eyes
And witnessed witnesses without alibis
Flesh vessels without spines bending like little rag dolls
I've seen godless women reign
Standing in courts, defending their name
While the law smirked at devils dressed in prayer shawls

I've seen innocent rightfully slain
And children singing on death trains
I've seen too much to hold within each eyeball
No spirit could my sight enthrall
I've grown so sick, my lids so tired
I convinced myself, I deserved some quiet
Of abrupt nature to nevermore see
And stop questioning what ought not be

No black nor white, no in-between
Perception short-lived, unforeseen
Crumbling bricks of an imposing stonewall
All bets set
When truth and time align to expose
Consequences no longer oppose
What I thought true, I deemed to be all
But I had seen nothing yet

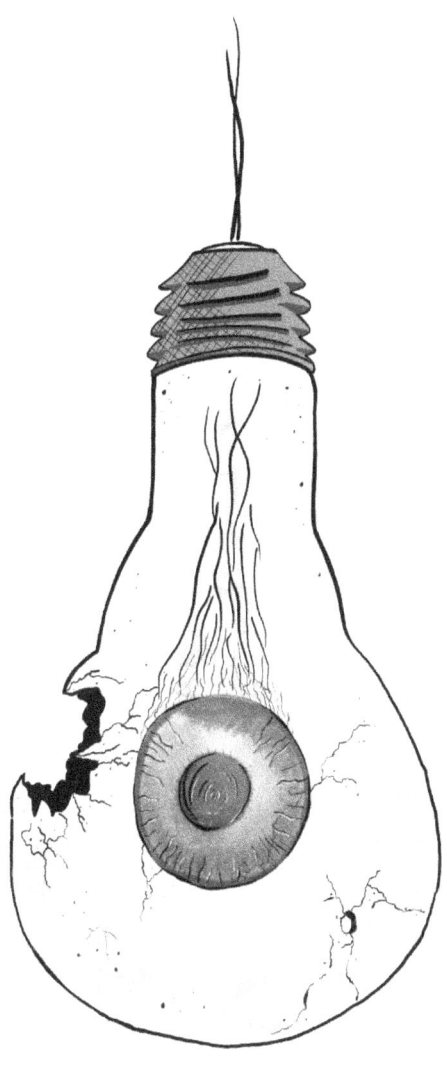

Before The First Touch

One touch
Reaching out
Through our painted faces
To lay our fingertips
On these vast places
So out of touch

And in connectivity
To read which in daily grind proceeds to withdraw
Even if only so much
Could this split second
Derange
And change
Then rearrange
These adopted roles
We continue to breathe
If only I could through this glimpse release
Reach you with ease
And install the same breath of faith
You provoked in me

If in one lifetime
We could make each other see
That which we dream about
Right here
Right now
At the first sight of newly infused life
The first glimmer of a fire no rain could pour down upon
Right here
Right now
Before the first touch
Before the first dawn
If you basked in the same golden suns as I
When in your presence
And felt caressed by the warmth of my hands as I
When stroked by your guarding eye
Why would we tremble
Before divinity in our embrace?

Quiet Skulked Upon The Hour

Quiet skulked upon the hour
Yearning, the privates within her bower
Lingering here in reveries
Desirous, lecherous memories
Of fondlings pervading
Dressed in lover's scent
Of eyes persuading
Dwelling in sweet torment

And as I crave for your soul to touch mine
I curse the lengthiness of time
As clearly time itself has played a trick
For when our bodies meet
The clock is rushing every tick

Thus I propose for us to venture
Away from norm and time and age
To lands of undiscovered pleasure
A blank line, an empty page
And feed on wild imagination
Committed to by word and pen
Until time's due narration
Permits you hold me close again.

Riptide

Can you count the shadows of my soul
When out of sight how would I ever know
If what I escaped has led you there
Can it be fate if we're not aware
Of each other's turns and twists in mind
Of dreams that were burnt and haven't returned to their kind
Of the afflictions and inhibitions we possess
Of the secret hopes we never confess…
But your voice constantly surrounds me
In your presence I spot what I could never see
Your touch is deeper than any wound I've harboured over time
Beside you I grow more sublime
Than what all my scars have taught me combined
I am yours.
And you are mine.
Like a dead star that keeps shining
I've blinded everyone.
Misled.
Fooled.
Everyone.
But you.
And you see past the disguise into the violent chaos

And hold the rage firmly but gently until it is still.
Ellipsis, aporia, pathos
Tracing the patterns until they rill
And you find the source
And touch the core
And the levee breaks
And the floods tear and pour
Riptide
At the mercy of armed might
Faith and fright
All collide

But your voice calms the roughest sea
'Grab onto me', I hear a soft whisper
Murmurs so far away
So low in pitch
Multichromatic in timbre
Soothing steadily
The melody of your words serenading me
Your eyes of candour alter the course
Your kisses caress the bruises of time
Lingering here I am yours
And as it proves you are mine.

Trailblazer

Tiptoeing until I become
Tiptoeing through life as it's fraying undone
I'm just passing by
No intention to stay
I've got no business with how you're wasting your life away

Unholy
Gold turning to rust
Unearthly rationalization
Out of your lines
I'm just passing by
Pharisee
No need to show me your hands
I know they're unclean

I'm your cautionary tale
Hidden away

Mistaken
You've got it all wrong
Thorn in the eye
Your lesson all along
You call yourself hunter
But I am not scared of you
I never was the prey
I'm only standing in your way
Pharisee

ANNINA MELISSA

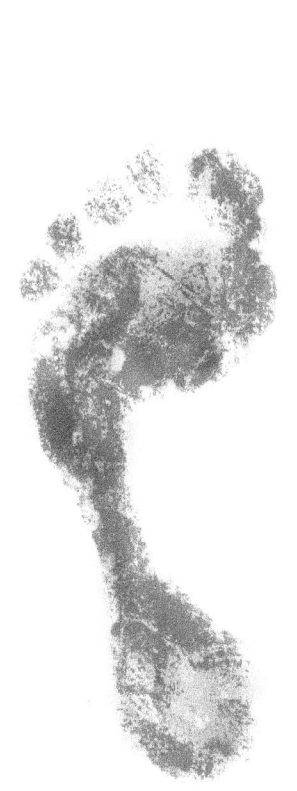

Sonder

Seeking in the stranger's gaze
Traces of comprehension
Eye on eye, reading through familiar haze
Across words we dare not mention

And as I escape to fathom ideas of sonder
These withering voices incite to ponder
The landscapes your mind might wander still
Absent from sight
Bent to your will
Kept in the garish soundness of thought
Hidden away from glimpses no one caught

Dot after dot
Climbing rock after rock
Sealed in the beholding
Of this watchful deadlock
As I'm following the steepness
Of my unpredicted ascending
Notion after notion
Of a mountain never-ending

But just as this restless rise peaks
The stranger's curiosity bluntly speaks
And I, on top of my introspection
Have no map to chart my direction
Every conclusion right in front of your stare
Yet none of them I lay bare

No effort in reason
Exposes the journeys we've taken
Still strangers to the eye
In complexity tied
But in reflection yet to awaken.

Echoes

My weapon of choice
Is the resonance of my voice

Driven as thousands have been before
Kindled in spirit, ignited at core
Rising up and raising for
I'd rather face than deliberately ignore

I found no joy in apathy
The bliss I tasted momentarily
Slipped through my fingers
Like breath I can't hold
All at my grasp
But not one thing to mold

No cause
No action
No power of own
Lethargy once sought refuge in
I've resoundedly overthrown

And here I walk in decades of echoes
Lighting the sparks in my voice
Against my own teachings
Against my beliefs
I've always had a choice

Firestarter

I am a firestarter
I am the Phoenix's daughter
I'm the witch in the flames you couldn't burn
I'm a firestarter
I was born to return

Just when the sparks have choked on glimmer
And rage and fury beneath your words simmer
Just when you thought all action's aborted
And no plot of yours could ever be thwarted
By one tiny grain of sand in the ocean
All gears have already been set in motion
Waves will simply swallow her up
Credibility gone, just tip her cup
But you were mistaken when weighing vows and
I am not one
We are thousands

Our disobedience
Is your inconvenience
They'd rather we scream in silence
Than speak about your crimes and violence
But time's running out
We have nothing to lose
Ever saw truth cut off
A man's hand dripping from abuse?

And one day in your prison cell
When you're looking back
Quietly you'll have to admit
You never thought she'd launch an attack
And be so courageous to believe her words
Would ever have weight in the courts of the world

We are firestarters
We are your most resilient daughters
We're the screams in the flames
You couldn't burn
It's our right to be heard
We were born to return

Horned Women

Fire-spitting
Fierce in nature
Eyes pacing past judging grins

Fervent spirits
Conceived in flames
We hold the suns within

Leaders and Warriors
Goddess
Enchantress
We set our paths ablaze

We're breaking down walls
We're birthing just rights
With horns that startle their gaze

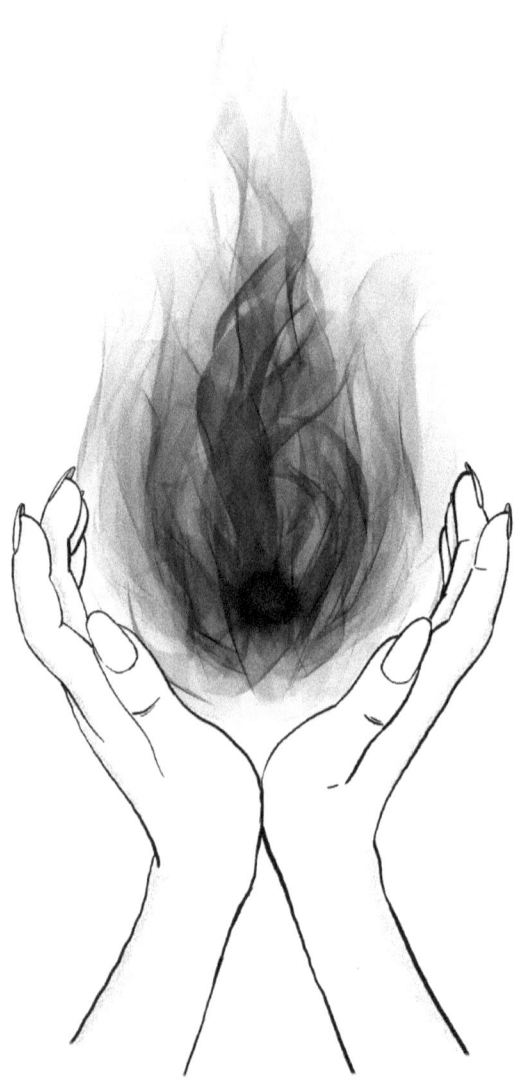

Shy Glimmers

Light is mere a glimmer shy
Daring to set off a spark
Within the innermost chambers belted
By bristling, stifling dark

Against all odds and words of wisdom
It carves its way past affliction
Unswervingly rekindling
Despite brute, malevolent prediction

Flickers raise inklings of faith
Not seen by eyes barricaded
For where there is no will to feast
All pursuit will perish unaided

So bask in the luster the darkness wraps tight
The purpose is yours to appraise
Then levitate these whispers of light
And set your life ablaze

Silent Waters

He doesn't know, but I see him.
Through the haze of cautious inflections and muzzled groans running dry over the same battered stories, acted out by the same delusive protagonist who comes and goes in fleeting faces.
Through the web of animosity, the mist of anguish, the gloss of bitterness - I can still see him.
I see the reflections of wholeness on the broken shards behind the vague smiles and restrained glimpses.
I see the prospect of entirety and expansion way beyond the limits of how we trained ourselves to define fortune, whenever he wraps his body around mine in the tight clasp of lovers, who for a split second disbanded their armor and allowed light to move on their naked skin.

I can see a crack in the shade.

Impossibility interrupted, hopelessness lifts its eyes to the sun orbiting the moon and the sky breaks open to spit out a sea of untamed implosions flooding the air we breathe.

And I stand here, motionless.

I'd rather brace the eye of the storm than drown in silent waters.
I won't let go. I'm not leaving.

I can see a crack in the shade.

Who numbed your tongue and deadened your voice?

I can see a crack in the shade.

Vertigo and fate - pointing in the same direction
we are falling
we are flying
we are falling
we are flying

I trust I saw a crack in the shade but how long before you dig out the abyss you can lapse into, if we're falling?

I won't let go. I'm not leaving.
And if my body hit rock bottom of my mind, I'd climb the same Impossibility again and take another leap until we've learnt to soar past the damage we've clinged to so eagerly.
If he'd only let me touch the wounds and sow the flesh and kiss the scars...
If only he saw what I see
he wouldn't let go.
He wouldn't leave.

Fears

I used to hold fears like rainy day friends
Close, center stage in my mind
Where events and constraints merge into each other
And plot ideas unrefined

The fear of madness, uncontrolled impulse
Insufficient renditions of existence amassed
Losing myself in grandeur of no value
The fear of failing at last

I used to fear men adorned in menacing sermons
In fact, I used to fear God
And also men armed with prescriptions
But more than anything, I feared my own thought

Not having answers when asked,
Explaining in vain against my urge,
A lack of purpose, at loss for words
Drowning in an inward surge
Of being mistaken at being alive
With no bonds to bear meaning
Holding lovers hostage
For my own hands not intervening

I once feared feeling good enough
And worthy in my skin
For fear of watching it slip through my fingers
Touching trophies without a due win

But fears did pass with lessons learnt
Yet this one I have earned
The only fear left cautiously
Is wasting time not being me

To Stand Tall When Feeling Small

To stand tall when feeling small
And stay quiet in your rhythm when prompted to express
To invent tools when expected to forge blades
To not swallow curses but instead choosing to bless

To raise faith in your words when delivering actions
And mean what you say day and night
To distinguish lies from integrity
Even when rolling from lips polite

And learning to love unconditionally
Finding happiness in solitude first
To conduct yourself with dignity
That no component of yours may feel coerced
Into never standing in your authenticity
Despite imperfection, although fond eyes grow sour
Make no room in your heart for hypocrisy
And above all else, own your power

ALL THE SHADOWS CAST LIGHT

Abalone

Sapphire skin
Wrapped around me tight
Layers thin
Wading through still moonlight
Primal sin
And lunar craze
Basking in
Your ample gaze

Hold me near
I'll hold you over
Paths unclear
Midst water clover,
Faith and fear
And spotted view
Rivers sheer
Of mortal hue
Euphoria carnal
Or holy communion
Lovers eternal
In sacred union

Azurite eyes
And abalone shell
Unparalleled prize
Ulterior spell
Sapphire skin
And rivers sheer
Caught me in
His surging sphere

Crystal clear
Bloom in the sun
Reappear
Where the streams run
Selenite
And touch come alive
Liquid light
Celestial dive

Brush Strokes

A work in progress
Substance untouched
A portrait yet to see

No mirror reflects
Your mind's exploration
Of all that you could be

No limits of thought
No enclosed expanse
Nor scaled-down boundaries

Where your mind resides
Prospect reveals
Infinite possibilities

Chances are plenty
No need to despond
When missions go amiss

Whatever you do
With this your life
I hope, you follow your bliss

I Only Run With Myself

Under wild moons
And tame skies
I only run with myself

In raging monsoons
Stripped off disguise
I only run with myself

Past kings and queens
Past dead and alive
I only run with myself

If all things were gone
This race is mine
I only run with myself

Völva

In deep, dark forests
The stellar dome
Clangs the wolves' howl
Guiding me home

Through barrier branches
And frail twigs
Dense foliage
And brittle sprigs
The soil beneath me
Grounded in woodland shawl
Moves my paces
Catches loose footfall

Sharp sight sees
Through nocturnal haze
Fearlessly
Rousing from daze
Of unearthly creatures
And auguries drear
Here in the wild
There's nothing to fear

Under starry scapes
Beneath orbit shine
The placid darkness I roam
Imposing shapes
And howls untwine
Granting
Chanting
Welcoming me home

Mother

In wisdom vast
In beauty unmatched
Boundless oceans of fondness

Love unsurpassed
Unconditionally attached
Solace
Priceless fortress

Admirers from every nation
Bearing witness to flawless creation
No words can make amends
For razing you gradually
Forging our own tragedy
Consuming past your defense

Far-flung roars
Pledge to restore
My heart twists at this loss
To worlds after worlds
You've given birth
Myriads of bridges to cross
For lovers
Explorers
Inventors akin
Affection compels to reclaim
There's no going back
There's no giving in -
Revolution in your name

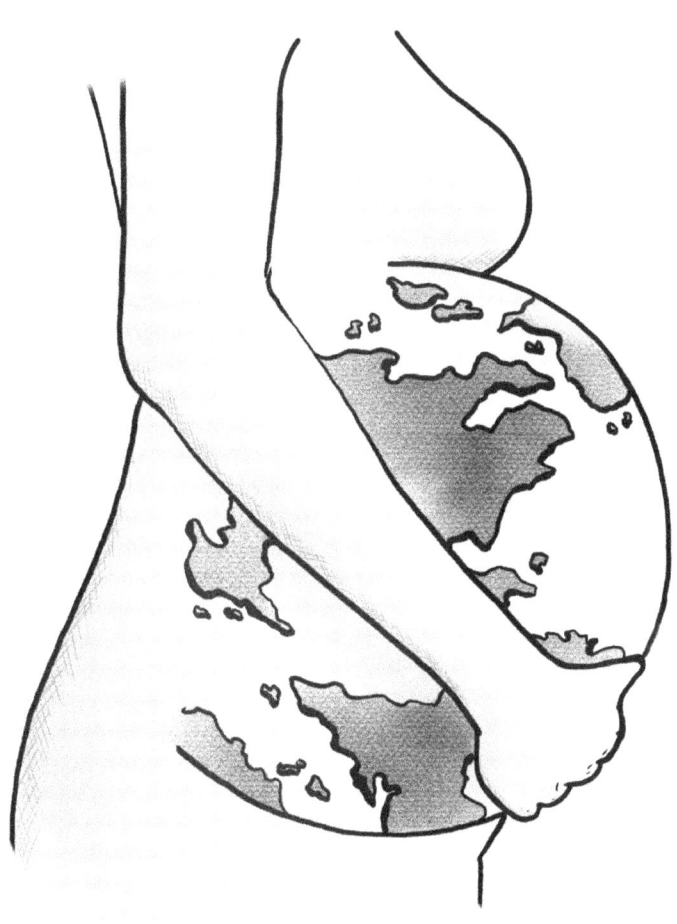

Ode To The Sea

Face of the ocean
With waters so deep
They swallow me whole
Like guiding lights
Embracing tides
Lead me to its resting soul
When mutually recognising
Your reflection in mine
As mine in yours
Hypnotising
These sightings and sweet musings intent
Are you and I born from the same element?

Effortlessly
I see
Beyond the hue
Of the ocean's crystal clear blue

No melody, no rhyme
Could frame this heart of mine
Or all that lies within
When your touch touches
And your kisses kiss
Words end where you begin

Yet if oceans held books
I'd unbury them in you
Vast riches
Embedded in vast blue

Yes, with heightened pleasure
I'd recover each treasure
And keep them guarded and safe
I'd scour all ruins
Outworn and fated
And brave the most somber caves
Even in shipwrecks long forsaken
I'd shine a light on gems no one's taken
And hold them dear in admiration
Mesmerised by their creation

In the most recondite depths of the sea
I've longed to sift through sand and debris
And know by heart each dream, every current
Closely observing his cadence fervent
As his waves tenderly wash over me
Ever immersed in the sea's boundless pulse
Breathing with each surge rhythmically
What moves the ocean, when does it convulse?

Below the surface drenched and soaked
Nothing compares to this lavish view
Adoration unrevoked
Devoting myself to the abiding blue

Solace is pouring from the quieting sound
Soothing each tantalising ideation
What I thought lost in his vision I've found
Dedicating without hesitation
Where one might drown in ventures askew
I descend and dive into the blue

Deserts I have wandered many
Landscapes I know how to roam
Yet constant drawn to the ocean's sweet call
Like a siren swimming home

Hourglass

How quickly time passes by
Our hourglass keeps turning
The numbers of age incline
For the lost sand we keep yearning

Faint memories start fading
But the taste of years remains
Slowly we're evaporating
As seasons shorten the reins

The youth of face has altered
The mind has widened its range
And though through pain it faltered
The soul does never change

Even if at times it was broken
Even if the heart froze cold
Deep within the truth is spoken
Sagacity will never grow old

But how foolish the notion of mankind
To stay held down by fears
The eyes we shut to blind
Ourselves from our own tears

Still this won't irritate time
Nor peels off the weight we bear
It walks its limitless line
It's ticking without a care

When The Marks Have Fallen

And when the marks have fallen from
What once sheltered this flesh
And nectar drips straight from your tongue
To allure and enmesh,
Enticed I let you strip my mask
From guard and caution bred,
Embrace this vulnerability
And wear my soul instead

Ahead

At odds with where my mind resides
I long for daylight after nights
Of bleakest timbres, unspeakable debt
There's no going back while moving ahead

I've travelled too far, I've fallen deep
I have fought countless ghosts
But who we are only begins to be
A journey unbeknownst

How to lead the fright in me
Lest it chained me down?
Ashes to ashes, rest for the dead
Weightless in prospect, look ahead

Rising within, so close at hand
My eyes feast on foreign murals
Boastful ideas, undiscovered lands
Remote from my memories rural
Exploration anew is worth the bet
Take the leap, go ahead

Comfort is a tragedy
Tainting the brightest potential
Paths will follow what daring eyes see
In visions reverential
Who would overlook a chance once met?
Don't hold back, keep looking ahead

Table of Contents
Darker Things

Quiet • 75

The Coutourier • 77

Dissolving Empires • 79

Unarmed • 81

Monachopsis • 83

I Don't Suppose You'd Understand • 87

When Left In Solitude • 89

Be Gone • 91

Burden • 93

Misanthropia - Act 1 • 97

Cracks • 99

Sweet Death's Calling • 101

Awake • 103

Dissociation • 107

On The Brink Of Death • 109

And Then I Was Running • 111
Empty Bottles For Empty Minds • 113
Sabotage • 117
The Forlorn • 123
Seers • 125
Electro Shock Girl • 129
Deracination • 133
Misanthropia - Act 2 • 135
The Sum Of Collapse • 137
How To Tame A Demon • 139
Holy Pied Piper • 141
In Irons • 145
Misanthropia - Act 3 • 149

Quiet

Words entangled
Dancing
Raving

Tongue is strangled
Misbehaving

Thoughts outpoured
But held so tight
Considered legions
Far from right

And in the clutter of expression
In my own withheld oppression
I give into my mind's riot
And say nothing
I stay quiet

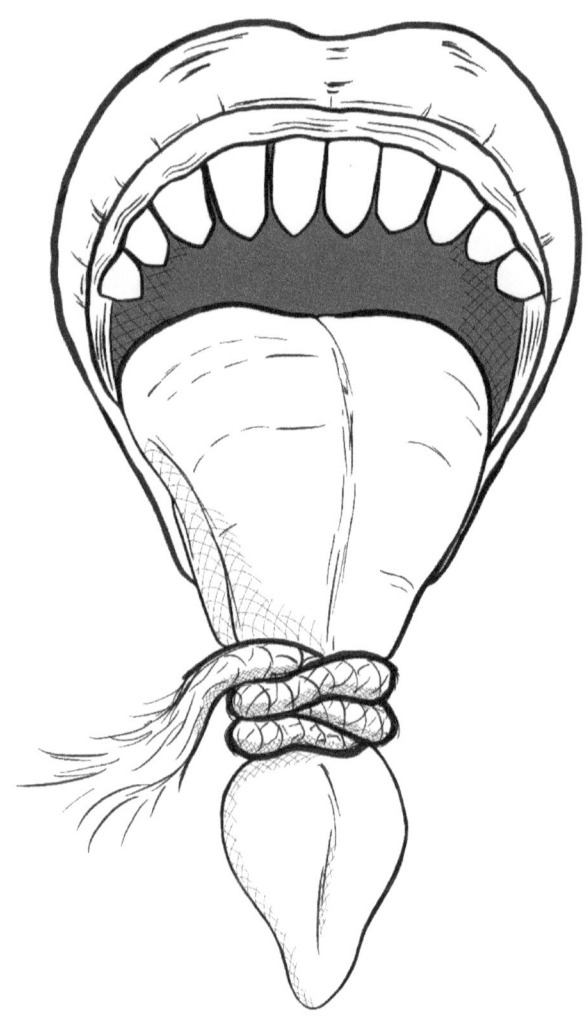

The Coutourier

Plots and impressions
Of stifling weight
Observant possessions
Ponderous bait

Overpowered and affected
On the surface uninfected
Mind from body disconnected
Inward by design

But when you ask about my pursuit
There is no fabric for this suit
I tailored in frenzy and so stay mute
'It's nothing. I am fine.'

Dissolving Empires

Silence is the reflection of our repugnancy after we've slain each other with the one persistent truth still burning under our coarse finger tips

I wanted to grab your hand and lead you away

Out of the improvident city and her screeching lights flickering on the inanimate bodies which squirm and writhe – boozed up – in pain their fears forbid to express

Beyond reach of conventional self-appointed experts and their presumptuous advice not asked for

Away from their shammed regimes incessantly bemusing our senses and twisting our system of values

Degradation
Abhorrence
Contempt
Scorn
untiring

But exactly as their respective subject, their targeted object you refuse to take it.
Systematically you've learnt to mistrust.
You've learnt that resistance in favour of your own beliefs is an onerous and secluded path.
You've learnt that whomever you lent the power to praise you has equal power to shatter.
But I am in no way superior to you.
My methods too are rooted in dissolving empires.

Silly boy.
If only you saw all you could be and reached out.

If only you dared to dive and cast your doubts away and detached yourself from a role thrust upon you so dutifully fulfilled all these years.

Maybe then we could leave this desolated place together assured of the indefinite prospects within our grasp.

Until then I'll serve as a reminder to you that broken bones are less painful than a bent back.

Unarmed

I have not meant to lose you
I cannot spare from harm
Along the path I was used to
Shriek awake from alarm
But the system started to fail
And I dared not to make a move
Of all the thoughts which prevail
I hardly have any proof

How can I not but mourn
Whatever led to this loss?
I am not innocent born
But I sure didn't know the cost

And in company I was so free
Before I crossed the line
But once you tripped
There's no guarantee
That you will return this time
So how shall I call this cold, dark place
The one so unfamiliar
I would so happily erase
If I knew how else to disbar

No words could ever explain
What has crushed my soul within
The demons each have their own name
I knew not what I was reeled in
I knew not how frantic I'd grow
Or how blood-dry I'd become
If the world turned just a little more slow
I wish it was burnt from the sun

So here I display my hatred
My anger
The will to kill
If all my words were rated
I'd be imprisoned still
But you have no need to fret
I beg you to stay calm
Against all the world's bet
I am almost unarmed

Monachopsis

Looking outside
But no one's looking in
Behind these towers of glass
The weight of your imprudent mass
Is starting to sink in

Winter's approaching
A patient and confident huntsman
His territory enclosing
Fear-struck more than
Any other prey I ran
Bewildered still
But clearer soon
Across the battle hill
Your many names were strewn

Under the willows
Where the wind will whisper premonitions
There's only one path
No peace for these wars of attrition

And under the willows
We lie spiritless and fallow
Behind our towers of glass
No one will dare to trespass

And it all just lingered a moment, Lover
Every voice agrees
Little do they know nor uncover
Some moments taint a lifetime with ease

If only you looked in
Before the shards erupted
And all sincerity wore thin
Maybe these our fortresses
Could have been reconstructed

But here I am the sole inhabitant
Of a landscape my eyes groan upon
The dweller of all things unattainable
While the moments have long gone

I Don't Suppose You'd Understand

The days pass by
The usual crime
Which reflects in my head
The memories won't die
You lie your lines
As I pretend you are dead
My anger is tamed
Hid well behind blame
My thoughts are no longer stuck
I cry out your name
I'm still unashamed
No, actually I don't give a …

Oh, gentlemen, come spit your blessings
And kiss your curses goodbye
'Cause off he ran to things most detesting
Don't ever ask me why
The answer is clear
It's simple to see
Guess I'm just out of luck
There's no time for fear
'To be or not to be'
So why should I even give a …?

'I know of your virtues
I know of your worth
I promise to love you indeed'
He sure knows he tortures
He can't see through the blurs
He can't even warm his cold feet

The hollow excuses
Your true vapid nature
Reveal the evil you tuck
Oh, still he refuses
The filth he recaptures
No, honestly I won't give a …

When Left
In Solitude

When left in solitude
Where all my thoughts unmute
Subduing sentiment
Aboding breaches never mend
There
Bracing in stillness
Not companion nor illness
Somewhere
There
Only I can end

When setting forth a journey of many miles
Where rekindled manners expedite courteous smiles
Quashing detriment
The ailment won't ever fend
The slowly rising notion
Then
Banned from all motion
Again
Then
Only I can end

And so
When gloom triumphs in bright sun beams
I cannot comprehend
The glow
In the room from your presence, it seems
Familiar
Why did we end?

Be Gone

Be gone
Be gone
Withered remotely
The blur in your gaze
The stain on my skin
Time's idle haze
And no era to linger in
And no tale to begin

Be gone
Be gone
With shallow winds
Where your bruise can't be traced
And names vanish like rotten carcasses
A bet mistakenly misplaced
Until the sight of bewrayment surfaces
A bleak lump of terrors without purposes

Be gone
Further away
Until the soil aches beneath your soles
And your mark will follow
Drain these fluids of life
Within my shell my shroud has long been hollow
Strip away the strife
No man washed up here stayed alive

Come, morbid Lover
Lay me to bed
Blow out the light
Cut the thread
Overcome me in certainty
That fear won't bail me out this time
Rest finally
To the melody of resolute chime
Untouchable eternally
That love won't remind me of vows
To the ashes peacefully
That passion won't awaken me now
Be gone
Be gone

Burden

Alas, my life - it's come to an end
I've tried to heed all advice
But depleted by torment I cannot pretend
The gain is not worth the price

Yes, the suffering is not worth living
The sum just won't add up
And all the love and faith I've given
Have shattered my already emptied cup

Each sunrise looks just the same
Each night fakes a death of routine
But the circles continue in vain
As I'm preparing to leave this churning machine
Yes, this factory of blood-soaked crimes
This pit of corrupting exhaustion
I'll finally act in accord to my rhymes
And cross the last clear caution

Don't warn me, loved ones, anymore
I've been alarmed enough
Certainty has draped my core
I'm handing in these cuffs

Mourn, my eyes, grieve for this loss
Paint my sight pitchblack
It takes just one fight to pay the cost
And I will never look back

And on the day I draw my last breath
I hope not to see your face
If only I desired you less
This growing conviction could not be erased

For this is the bond, the burden of mine
To always listen for your voice
Through all of our shame I held you divine
No, hope hasn't left me a choice

Now don't you weep or break or cry
I've gone to slumber deep
And in this relief I peacefully lie
Believe me, I'm only asleep
Yes, in this darkness my life's been untied
It's freed me - I'm only asleep
I found another light way to fly
Believe me - I've stopped to creep.

Misanthropia - Act 1

It's not your fault
In their ignorance you were taught
Reckless abomination
Non-existent hesitation
Rapacious
Ostentatious
Greedy, little feeble-minded
Eating yourself alive
Of all virtues deprived
Atrocious
Wallowing in your own hypnosis
I am lost to this world

CRACKS

Now need I not put my faith together
Confronting rotten society?
What is held proudly and called oh so clever
Has turned out to be dressed in cruelty
And as they spin and laugh
And forget their crimes
I feel my voice is sinking
The screams grew more silent
Each tormentful time
Swallowed by plighted thinking

Need I also call plots games?
Feel my dignity erased?
See the cowards join the crowds
Which never care for strapped truth's shouts
Which ran in fright but bravery
Through sickly repeated centuries

But small man, good man
Will not demand
To put all this nonsense
To a veered end
Not one fool will take
Courage and stand
Against the so-felt feeding hand

And so they scratch and bite
Each average night
Each other's average face
And they poked the right's eye
Hoping it becomes blind
At least to this average case

And here I sit and stare in certainty
At all the cracks in humanity
And all the pieces that won't rearrange
What good is faith if there's no change?
And why beat the heart if there's no rest?
But no soul is barred
From this failed quest

Sweet Death's Calling

Sweet Death's Calling
In the middle of my fright
Dragging life's attention away
Screaming in the spotlight

Bottle up tears
Fast forward the years
And see if it all was worthwhile
Will you ever catch a glimpse
Of what's beyond the brim
Of hollow eyes and a styrofoam smile?

I'll forgive and forget
Stillborn from regret
But neglected I have my promise
To live to the end
Past inviolable defense
Yet the will to do so I miss

Still, you pull under cover
Your mighty, manly hand
The reason I've discovered
They'll never really understand
That what once escaped the eye
Has ceased to exist
Lost between consciousness
And intangible, luminous mist

No, truth cannot be battled
Then who are you to try?
My visions are still shackled
Will death whisper to me a lullaby?
Calm down these aroused senses
And hush my nightmares away?
The most costly of expenses
But if in peace, I will pay
Even when my tongue is cursing
And my body's out of mind
Even if the act's rehearsing
Loses meaning in this plight

Oh, those poor, captured insomniacs
Who don't hear the alarm clocks roaring
I'll bend my ear, wipe off my fear
To listen to a new daze calling

Awake

Thee I call my enemy
My foe, wicked fiend
Thy claws are longing
Waiting in patience for me

Is it more fun to slit my dreams
Than to burst anyone else's?
When you caught me between the seams
Pulling daggers with a gleam
Disappearing in arcane steam
Who will care for the knell's
Solitary, drowning cry?
Who will curse? And who will spy?
Cross their lives out with thine eye
Fade their breath with one sweet sigh

Ah, dearest murderer
Thou can't tiptoe near me
Overrated, painted fate
In the dark I've learnt to see
In the pit of widened skies
Deadened in the twist of night
Guess my life is still at stake
I shall better stay awake

Oh, heartbeat's racing, chasing, roaring
Taking over my thoughts pouring
Constantly, heavily down on my soul
Thunders and lightnings out of control
And they tore and ate the obliging coward
Gain from this scene
Let my mind devour
That rest has scratched us all but skin-deep
Watch your back 'ere you fall asleep

So once the spotlight vanishes
And the whole world hides away
I cannot as well be foolish
In slumber I am preyed

But with each passing day
My eyes turn itchy and dry
By no means I could obey
For when I shut them I will die

Close in on me, you tormentful nights
All the screaming
The bleeding
The gore
I've choked on my dreamings,
Survived on my frights
So you won't harm me no more

Insomniatic, fearful host
How thy spirits shake
I'm haunted by these nightmares' ghosts
Again, once more I'll stay awake

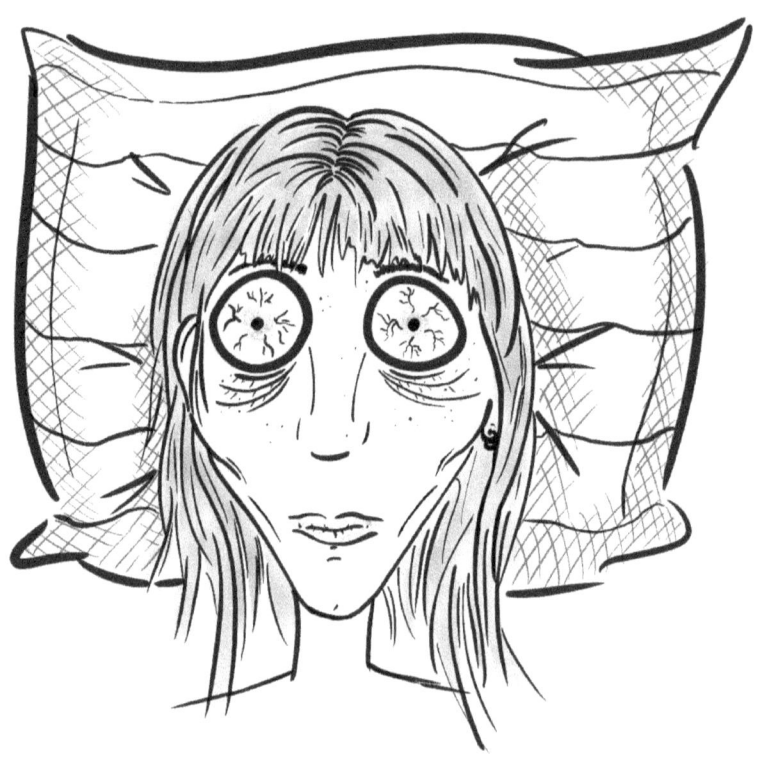

Dissociation

Words that aren't mine
Voices shivering down my spine
Breach of thoughts
Existence in schisms
Valueless terms
Vague euphemisms
Sought to decode
Terrors of reason
Sensory overload
Within me treason
State of emergency
Abnormal fugues
Loss of identity
Trauma incused
Therapy sessions
Pills to forget
Sincere confessions
Beaded regret
Words that are muted
Voices implode
Thoughts disputed
Existential overload

On The Brink Of Death

Even in hours cheerful and jolly
Even in fancy, even in folly
I feel a breeze
I hear a breath
I'm still on the brink of death

Even when reserved I reached out
And left all fears behind
Although I commanded myself not to doubt
The light is never bright

My eyes are blurred
From distant worlds' hurt
You see what you perceive
A whisper keeps echoing
Screaming
Entangling
'One cut and you'll be relieved'

No.

'One step – your heart will be at ease'

No.

'Admit at last, you can't even breathe!
Have you forgotten how dull existence is?'

No.

'Don't fool yourself with man-made cures
Or prayers to prolong the fall!
You can't quiet the truth
Or shush me away,
Cause inside your mind
I am installed.'

Even in the lightest hours
Even when in greatest powers
I can feel its choking sphere
I can hear it drawing near
Unnoticed by everyone surrounding
It stares at my blood-shot heart pounding
Digging its claws into my veins
Drowning my body in its filthy stains
Poisoning, stabbing me with its foul breath:
'Give in, bravest, you're on the brink of death.'

And Then I Was Running

And then I was running
I was running so fast my feet barely touched the ground
And moments shot passed me in the blink of an eye
Too blurry, too messy to ponder on
What a waste of time
Detecting
Deciphering
Limiting
I can't stop
I'm running
I'm thriving
I'm so close to flying
I'm so close to running my feet into the wide skies
So close to taking flight
Just focus
Don't look right nor left
Past broken hearts
Unmended Bonds
Meaningless rides
Meaningless time
Meaningless lines as the lines of time ride their traces into my skin

And I can't recognise this face observing me from afar
like a shadow clinging to mornings gone
Following my every step
I was running towards horizons
Now I'm running from you
The blank void
The traces
The face that won't stop staring as I'm running
And running
And running

Empty Bottles For Empty Minds

No need to scream
We're done before
The nurses tie you to the floor
Your troubling mind is picturesque
What beautiful experiments
We are compelled to exercise
The outcome is our grand surprise
Electro shocks to humanise
Your body slowly tranquilised
No touch is felt
Your vision blurred
Along with pleasure
We've numbed hurt
These pills are made
From blood and dross
Wild muscle spasms
Memory loss
Tunnel eyes
And dried up tongues
Weight in water
Stifled lungs

Out of body
Emptied minds
Side effects
Of special kinds
Jagged ideas
Straighter jackets
Warning signs
In square brackets
Insanity in spotlight
Doc, set the stage!
Bars on each window
Locked in this cage
Of no perspectives
And syringe gods
No escaping
These metal rods

Little Miss Bipolar
Caught a fever
Saw most magical things
Mind weaver
Flew too high
Then fell to low
Raving prescriptions
On the go

Her mind is too adventureous
How dare she think so scandalous?
Let's squash and squeeze her into form
Till she behaves just like the norm

Confrontations required
Injections plenty
Success rate states
Almost one in twenty
More Lithium
Highly concentrated
Oops! Our bad
She's intoxicated!
Dysfunctional and debilitated
Her mind yet outstandingly moderated
No will to live
Just as before
Triumphant defeat
Of her visions galore
More pills to feed
No rest assured
For the poor lives of
Mentally uncured

And this, clever one, is the universal curse
To doubt incessantly, which affliction is worse.

Sabotage

I speak in rhymes
Of frantic designs
My mind is never still

I tend to explore
What most choose to ignore
I'm a scientist in my world, if you will

But once stableness ponders
And knocks on my door
I can't open but wonder
What life was before

All steps must be theorized
And carefully adjusted
All processes sterilized
And precisely conducted
Every possibility must be calculated
Every flaw, defect or error accurately rated

What's motionless must be moved
All notions must always improve
The cycles are there to be broken
Poor humanity has still not woken

I speak in dreams
Of cracking seams
Until a green stem follows

My chaos tears off
All which can be stuffed I shove
And all the rest I swallow

Once I'm seized by the flow
My body's out of control
And so no longer master

Thought after thought
Eyes racing - idea bought
I am rushing ever faster

And one morning when I rose
To angels singing in my ear
I realised that I was God
And suddenly it all was clear

There's no impossibility
But no one is aware
Apart from maybe only me
In that case, why not lay it bare?

No inhibition
Free admission
Blurred lines of perception

Grandiosity
Lost prophecy
Chosen for conception

I am swept away by playful art
I've been so ever from the start
Ingenious acts delight my heart
Purifying, I might stress

But the world won't join in my revolt
Most sprang from untaught, I've been told
Views range from 'nonsense' to 'nothing but cold'
I'm sorry, again I digress

How can I make it short and clear?
I sabotage myself, I fear

I've not uncovered the full extent
But I'll think it over until I bend
And suspect I'm never free to be
The secret agent of my alchemy
A mad girl's vocation
Erratic dilation
An unmuzzled brain which serves me constriction
Judges in white cloaks declare my conviction
Reality's exposed
But it's not what I see
Why open my eyes
If there's no way to be?

Yes, whenever there is clarity
And I steer towards certainty
My drives can't seem to set or rest
And distrust invades to manifest

I've walked the line a million times
It never felt more real
Against my own a list of crimes
I sabotage myself, I feel

An abundance of betrayal
Committed in disguise
It seems I've set the sail
I'm feeding myself lies

If only I could decipher
And distinguish truth from pretense
I'd probably not suffer
From concluding that nothing makes sense

It's a strange pact, staying alive
The credit is mine to forego
If it's ever worth all the strife
I suppose, I'll never know

The Forlorn

Show me where the forlorn congregate
Hidden deep in the forest
Where your roots have led me before
Curious feet heed the calling
Of the long lost, whispering moor

All sanguine streams
Cry from beneath
Begging for remembrance
Surge of souls
Armed with scrolls
Waiting for their ascendence

I've heard all the stories
The legends, the tales
The myths, the lore and the fear
Intertwined conclusions
Dissenting allusions
Diffuse
Between fabrics sheer

Bring the unforgiven to life
Breathe - we are reliving their plight
Before the day's arising
Unstring the dawn from its creatures
Before the dark's advancing
I'll bear you amongst my treasures

SEERS

There were signs.
I swear there were signs.

I'm a ball of thread imploding.
Strung the wrong way.
And it all collapses silently, without a sound,
Without a noise for anyone to bend their ear.

Vision failed. Mission failed.

I am nothing but a tick ruling over every move.
This journey was never real, born from deceit…
Consequences are a bitter reminder of nescience.
I am trapped in an hourglass I never believed to exist,
A coil I was tricked into denying.
I am a moth eaten by your flames, but it doesn't matter because I only had one day to live anyway.
But nobody told me.
Nobody told me.

And I juggle the blame like your God juggles life –
incalculable and terrifyingly abrupt.

There must have been signs. Written all over the fuming stratosphere, screaming at me from the slammed, forbidden doors, engraved in the bed I lay myself to sleep in after days were done, after all days are done after days after days after days after days after I remember to sleep and wish not to wake but I do and I cringe and wreathe 'God! Why I when millions die night after ride after ride?!' and I pluck my head and clean the cobwebs from my heart but all the lines I draw cripple like old rumours rolling off my shoulders.

'It's a vanity', they say. No need to understand or question.
If only I unplugged my brain as the common do
and just switched off and ignored I'd exult from this overload of amputated bliss.
I'd hail every action ensuring these disastrous ramifications as long as it allays the tiniest hint of suspicion and lulls me into believing my own ignorance is superior to any physical law.
I'd distract myself with poor complacency and belittling pleasures.
And I'd be at ease.

Fully absorbed in a whitewashed world too
impoverished to question,
too garish to see.

But I can't. I implode.
I see this jarring parade and blow chunks from my
deepest dells of woe and contumely.
What a howling theatre!
What disgraceful actors!
What a preposterous play.

'God! Why I, when millions die night after stride after
stride?'

But there are no signs. No guidance.
Strung the wrong way and it all collapses silently,
without a sound, without a cry or whisper or scratch for
anyone to bend their tin ears.

In their deafness I am mute.

Electro Shock Girl

I'm the dark
Eating every spark
Alive
I'm the dead
Killing what is bred
With knives
Made of broken promises
And shattered, poisoned dreams
You're running from farther
You're bleeding, oh mother
Is it ever what it seems?

I'm the girl behind the mirror
Waiting to infect
Guess you never saw me clearer
But I'm not all that you suspect

Electro shock blues
Just a little spasm rhyme
And I am reborn new
Swirling to the chime
Of blissful new memories to come
Forget all the hurt
Forget how undone
And torn I used to be
The little porcelain face
But wait
The cracks aren't gone
The pain is not erased

All the psycho pills of the world
Couldn't make her a happier girl

I'm the dark
Eating every spark
Alive
I'm the thunder
Is it any wonder
I took your life?

Deracination

I trace your blood to the seed
An accumulation of laments planted eras ago
Where Zeitgeist is demanding its toll
And I've become a product of another failed breed

I am the executor of my heritage's insignificance
I chopped down my lifeline to provide unmistaken evidence
No justifications
No return, no allegations
The roots bleed
My eyes breached

She's taking over

A judge to the shredded leaves
Fallen pale and dead
Let me inform her Majesty
Her kingdom is all wrecked
My shade will swallow all her light
Until her porcelain face
Smashes against her fateful pride
To diminish and erase

Misanthropia - Act 2

Ease my scarred mind
My abductive inference
Is merely adherence

I become what my eyes are fed
Am I whole yet?
Devoid of these holes yet?

Always seeking
Connecting, bleeding
I don't speak your frame of mind
Meet my devils
Judges dishevelled
Take apart and crucify

The Sum Of Collapse

He pulled at his hair like wires hanging loose
Frenzy dancing, atom-melting
Desynchronized in a world that just about made sense at a glance
If observed through bleary oculars
Sights halting,
Vision-forming
Pull away but they invade the words hummed in your sleep,
The years gone missing,
The corners of those lazy eyes
You're a subject to a spectacle only witnessed from the spotlight.
Now aren't you special?
With no one to imprint sense on, how can you be certain?
When you raise between rigidity and ritual the ghosts of past convulsions, what are they saying you haven't already told yourself?
Why do you listen?

She plucked the shards from her skin like crystals embedded in crimson rivers. Shimmer by shimmer.
Where's your shame? Whose forgiveness will you whimper?
Childish pastimes to evade the hammer strokes of an unattainable view.
Concave silhouettes, fading figures. Only a phase.

There's the jury we fall prey to.

How many useless roads could I have been prevented from walking down, had I known that the sum of collapse bears little weight on my own immediate perspective?
Each to their own burden. Each to their own story.
And how many distraught nights could I have saved myself from, when neon lit writings in unsuspected alleyways proclaimed
'Healing knows no linearity'
And I had believed them?

How To Tame A Demon

How to tame a demon?
That can be quite arduous
For some have a rather indiscernible nature
Whereas others grab you by your throat with their withy talons and spill their acrid poison up your unsuspecting ear, where it nests, patiently, until it's poised to attack.

You wouldn't know what had occupied the space inside your mind, where time stretches and shrinks like unruly visions brought vividly to life by your frenzied eyes

Manic Delerium
Lunar Stare
Feral madness
Damage beyond measure
Beyond words
Beyond repair

She knew her demons. They exchanged frequently. And when they screamed, she let them exhaust themselves until their hoarse voices stifled any urge to interact. But when they spoke, she listened with such focussed intent as that of an adept warrior studying each and every angle of the proposed battlefield. Except she wasn't at war.

Insane, bright lunacy
Damage control

How to tame a demon?

No one knows for sure
'It's quite arduous', she said

'But I'm no longer afraid of people, or monsters hiding under my bed
Because all the monsters gather together right here in my head.'

Holy Pied Piper

Good little boys and girls
Good little boys and girls
Good little, trusting, bearing boys and girls
Joyous
Unassuming
Like little lambs playing
With the wolf in disguise
Grooming - just a matter of time
Looming - just a matter of turning blind eyes

Run

God is your shepherd
You shall not speak
He will make you sit on filthy laps
Holy chambers
Minor traps

He will drown you in stifled screams
And lead you into the lecherous hands
Of the wicked for his name's sake

'God is my shepherd
I shall not speak
Though I walk through the valley of the shadow of death
He leads me in the paths of righteousness'

I know you are listening
Murderer
Safe in your unimpeachable, watchful towers
Murderer
The virtueless sinful
Leading the faithful
Knuckling under your almighty power
Blasphemous preaching
Imbecile teaching
'In God's hands lay it bare!'

Thorn in your spiritual eye
An unworldly flock
Of consecrated judges against one witness
The truth you've conjured
Upon countless, good little boys and girls
Has even left the devil witless
Undetected
Dark figure
Unreported crime

Sacrifice me
Strip me of all credibility
In the name of the one true God
Who is refuge to the predators
That bribe your halls of worship
For confidential oaths of silence
- Dare tell me I'm wrong
As I sit across from your deflection
Vague shadows in the gaslight
Fate of heresy
And threats of impending doom
Scales in your fist
Weighing life against voice

I stopped being scared, brothers.

I stopped being scared
When I discovered
Your formulated conscience never skips a beat
After all - what might man do to me
God hasn't already permitted?

Good little boys and girls
Good little boys and girls
Shredded to pieces
By wolves in the spotlight

ALL THE SHADOWS CAST LIGHT

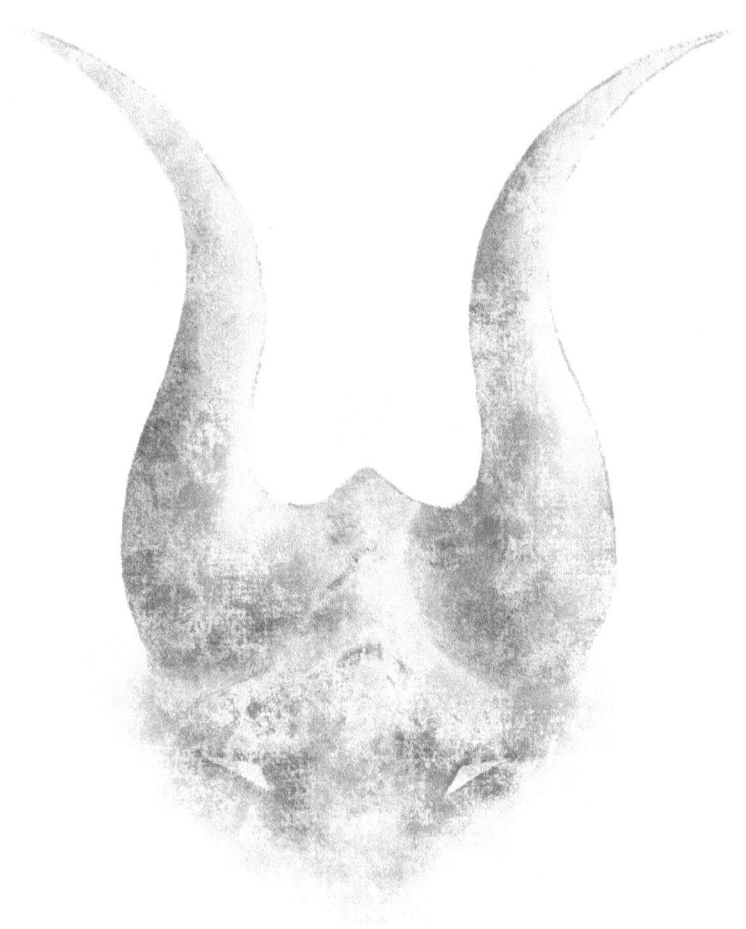

In Irons

Keep calm – and watch the forced perspective throbbing repeatedly
Past our muted skin
Sharp screams – bright as stars
As clouds commence plotting secretly
What the dark bred within
But once the veil is lifted
And the focus clear
My perception is shifted
I stop to wander
I set to steer
This ringing in my head
Killed over and over by the same hands
Shushed and silenced
By the same tides
The same reprimands…
Still this stinging isn't dead
Suppressed and withheld
Choked until unfelt
Stabbed and strangled
Buried alive
Right and wrong entangled
Until the pangs subside
Until the loss doesn't spring to my mind

Until I feign the disillusions decline
Time after time after time….
Have I betrayed my ideals?
Always searching – never finding
And traded providence for a bland sop?
Always connecting – never confiding
Once I cross the horizon
There is no reversion
No limits to this scope
Then is there no courage without fear?
I stop to wander
I set to steer
Keep calm – and don't blink twice
Keep quiet –the fight is not worth the price

Bottled-up and buttoned-down
Bread and circuses to appease the frowns
And merry-go-rounds to deflect from our own dehumanization
Contaminating each and every generation

Still these sirens absorb the calls of your thirst for power
And with every mile I sail your inflicting doubts I will devour
Debilitate the shame
Redirect the blame
I will take back control
Retrieving all you ever stole

And when you lie upon your earned attaint
And pride forbids to heave a sigh
I'll dispatch a whisper
A signal faint
Keep calm – the end is nigh

Misanthropia - Act 3

Fearless and faceless
I'm falling into the abyss
Eyes wide
Chided child
Transgressing into the light
I feel your hollowness
Suiting me in the process

Confess
Confide
Reverse catharsis
Confess
Confide
Trapped in psychosis
Confess
Identify
Empty your carcass

It's not your fault
Run away before you're caught

I remember when the days seemed so long
And I certainly, certainly knew right from wrong
I knew where this flesh of mine belonged
I knew I'd never falter
Like people in waves around me
I toss and turn each way
Divinity, surround me
Epiphany, illuminate me
Disrupt me
Construct me

If you are in emotional distress or thinking about suicide, help is available.
You are not alone.
If you are in immediate danger, please call your local emergency number (such as 112 in Europe, 999 in the UK, or 911 in the US).
Below are free and confidential crisis helplines in several countries.
Most are available 24 hours a day.

United Kingdom & Ireland
Samaritans – Call 116 123 (freephone)
Shout (text) – Text SHOUT to 85258

United States
988 Suicide & Crisis Lifeline – Call or text 988
Crisis Text Line – Text HOME to 741741

Australia
Lifeline Australia – Call 13 11 14
Suicide Call Back Service – Call 1300 659 467

Canada
Talk Suicide Canada – Call 1-833-456-4566 or text 45645 (4 pm–midnight ET)

Germany
TelefonSeelsorge – Call 0800 111 0 111 or 0800 111 0 222
telefonseelsorge.de (online chat)

France
3114 – Call 3114 (24/7, free)

Italy
Telefono Amico – Call 02 2327 2327

Spain
Línea 024 – Call 024

Netherlands
113 Zelfmoordpreventie – Call 113 or 0800 113 0 113

Switzerland
La Main Tendue / Die Dargebotene Hand – Call 143

India
Aasra – Call +91 9820466726

Worldwide
Befrienders Worldwide – befrienders.org
Find a Helpline – findahelpline.com

www.ingramcontent.com/pod-product-compliance
Lightning Source LLC
Chambersburg PA
CBHW040245010526
44119CB00057B/826